Harold R Foster

Prince Valiant

COMPRISING PAGES 47 THROUGH 92

The Singing Sword

FANTAGRAPHICS BOOKS

ABOUT THIS EDITION:

Produced in cooperation with the Danish publisher Interpresse and several other publishers around the world, this new edition of *PRINCE VALIANT* is intended to be the definitive compilation of Hal Foster's masterpiece.

This volume collects, in the most affordable and handsome format yet, the second 46 pages of the Sunday strip. Also available from Fantagraphics Books are six more collections of Foster's *Prince Valiant* work (Vols. 1, 27-31). Future releases will continue reprinting the earlier material (from 1938 through the end of the 1950s); once the series has "caught up" with its earlier releases, those will be reprinted, or (if they are still in print) skipped in order to complete the collection with the final era (late 1960s through 1982, when Foster handed over the strip to John Cullen Murphy). The ultimate goal is to have all 40 volumes in print simultaneously, making available the entirety of Hal Foster's 45-year epic.

ABOUT THE PUBLISHER:

FANTAGRAPHICS BOOKS has dedicated itself to bringing readers the finest in comic book and comic strip material, both new and old. Its "classics" division includes the ten-volume *The Complete E.C. Segar Popeye* and the monthly *NEMO: The Classic Comics Library*. Its "modern" division is responsible for such works as Yellow Kid Award-winner *Love and Rockets* by Los Bros. Hernandez, Peter Bagge's *Neat Stuff*, the American edition of José Muñoz and Carlos Sampayo's *Sinner*, and *The Complete R. Crumb*. See the back cover for a complete listing.

PREVIOUS VOLUMES IN THIS SERIES:

PRINCE VALIANT, Volume 2
»The Singing Sword«
comprising pages 47 (January 1, 1938) through 92 (November 13, 1938)
Published by Fantagraphics Books, 1800 Bridgegate Street Suite 101, Westlake Village, CA 91361
Editorial Co-Ordinator: Helle Nielsen
Colored by Montse Serra
Cover inked by Gorm Transgaard and colored by Søren Håkansson
Fantagraphics Books staff: Kim Thompson & Doug Erb
Copyright © 1987 King Features Syndicate, Inc., Bull's, Interpresse, and Fantagraphics Books, Inc.
Printed in Italy
ISBN 0-930193-47-4
First printing: Summer, 1988

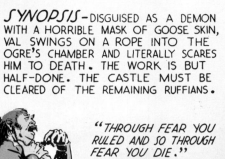 

Prince Valiant

IN THE DAYS OF KING ARTHUR
BY
HAROLD R. FOSTER

SYNOPSIS—DISGUISED AS A DEMON WITH A HORRIBLE MASK OF GOOSE SKIN, VAL SWINGS ON A ROPE INTO THE OGRE'S CHAMBER AND LITERALLY SCARES HIM TO DEATH. THE WORK IS BUT HALF-DONE. THE CASTLE MUST BE CLEARED OF THE REMAINING RUFFIANS.

"THROUGH FEAR YOU RULED AND SO THROUGH FEAR YOU DIE."

NO ACTOR COULD HAVE STAGED HIS DRAMATIC EFFECTS BETTER THAN DID VAL DURING THAT NIGHT OF HORROR.

WRAPPED IN HIS BLACK CLOAK HE IS INVISIBLE IN DARK CORNERS, BUT HIS SUDDEN APPEARANCES ARE FRIGHTFUL TO THE OGRE'S HENCHMEN.

HIGH AMONG THE RAFTERS OF THE DINING-HALL, VAL SITS THROUGH THE LONG DAY, HUNGRY AND THIRSTY, WAITING FOR DARKNESS AND HIS FINAL ACT.

WHEN DARKNESS FALLS THE FRIGHTENED OUTLAWS SEAT THEMSELVES IN THE DINING-HALL, BUT NOT FOR LONG. WITH A SCREAM THE DEMON SAILS OUT OF THE DARKNESS ACROSS THE TABLES AND DISAPPEARS AGAIN.

SWINGING UP TO THE BALCONY ACROSS THE HALL VAL WATCHES THE CONFUSION BELOW

47 1-1-38

IN THEIR FEAR THEY RUSH TO THEIR MASTER, BUT FIND HIM DEAD WITH NO SIGN OF A WOUND!

—NEXT WEEK—
"PANIC!"

SYNOPSIS:
WITH HIS HORRIBLE MASK PRINCE VALIANT HAS FRIGHTENED THE OUTLAWS INTO PANIC. RUSHING TO THEIR FEARFUL LEADER THEY FIND THE OGRE UNWOUNDED, BUT STONE DEAD.

A TERROR WHO CAN BRING DEATH THUS IS MORE THAN EVEN THESE HARDENED OUTLAWS CAN STAND.

AND SOON THE MORE TIMID ARE HURRYING FROM THE GLOOMY CASTLE.

AS DAY DAWNS VAL WATCHES THE GROWING PANIC WITH SATISFACTION.

SOON THE WHOLE BAND IS RUSHING MADLY FROM THE HAUNTED CASTLE.

LOOKING BACK THEY CAN SEE AN OMINOUS BLACK FIGURE WATCHING THEIR FLIGHT.

HAL FOSTER 48 1-8-38

"*THAT'S THAT!*" SAYS VAL, QUITE PLEASED WITH THE SUCCESS OF HIS TRICK AND REMOVES THE OILY GOOSESKIN MASK.

NEXT WEEK—"CORNERED"

SYNOPSIS:
THINKING ALL THE OUTLAWS HAD FLED IN TERROR, VAL REMOVES THE HORRIBLE MASK, BUT TWO HARDY RUFFIANS, DELAYED BY THEIR SEARCH FOR LOOT, DISCOVER HIM AND HIS TRICK.

THE ARMED THIEVES ADVANCE, GRINNING FIENDISHLY.

BEING UNARMED, VAL SEEKS SAFETY IN FLIGHT.

THE OUTLAWS CORNER HIM, BUT HE REMEMBERS HIS ROPE DANGLING OUTSIDE AND LEAPS FROM THE WINDOW—

SWINGS FAR OUT AND CLAMBERS UPWARD.

ONE RUNS TO THE ROOF WHILE THE OTHER WAITS AT THE WINDOW.

49 1-15-38

AND DEATH COMES VERY CLOSE TO THE YOUNG PRINCE AS HE SWINGS BACK AND FORTH HELPLESSLY.

—*NEXT WEEK*—
"THE HUMAN TARGET"

49

SYNOPSIS — VAL'S TRICK CLEARS THE CASTLE OF OUT- LAWS, BUT HE IS DISCOVERED BY TWO WHO REMAIN BE- HIND FOR LOOT—AND IS PUR- SUED TO THE ROOF WHERE HIS SITUATION BECOMES DESPERATE.

WITH CRUEL DELIBERATION THE OUTLAW SLOWLY SAWS AT THE SLENDER ROPE.

SWINGING INWARD VAL JUST MANAGES TO GRASP A SUPPORT IN TIME.

WHILE HIS ENEMY IS STRIVING TO REACH HIM WITH HIS SWORD, VAL MAKES A NOOSE.

WHICH HE SUDDENLY FLIPS UPWARD.

AND EASILY JERKS HIM SCREAM- ING FROM HIS POSITION.

WHILE VAL SLOWLY DRAWS HIM UPWARD, THE NOOSE SLIPS---

50 1-22-

--AND THE CAPTIVE PLUNGES TO THE GROUND.

BUT THE SECOND OUTLAW HAS REACHED THE COURTYARD AND SHOUTS UPWARD, "HERE'S HOW WE HUNT SQUIRRELS IN SINSTAR WOODS."

"POOR SQUIRRELS," MUTTERS VAL, WONDERING HOW LONG HE CAN DODGE THESE WHISTLING MESSENGERS OF DEATH

NEXT WEEK — THE DUEL OF WITS

SYNOPSIS:
CORNERED UNDER THE EAVES BY THE REMAINING OUTLAW, VAL IS A TARGET FOR A FLIGHT OF SCREAMING ARROWS—IT SEEMS BUT A MATTER OF TIME BEFORE ONE BRINGS HIM CRASHING TO THE COURTYARD BELOW.

REMOVING CLOTHING, THE YOUNG PRINCE TIES HIS GARMENTS IN A BUNDLE WHICH HE USES AS A SHIELD.

UNABLE TO REACH HIM FROM ABOVE OR BELOW, THE OUTLAW PLANS VAL'S DOOM CAREFULLY. HE REMOVES ALL THE WEAPONS FROM THE TOP FLOOR.

LOCKING THE DOORS SO VAL CAN NOT ESCAPE. HE LIGHTS THE SIGNAL BRAZIER.

WHEN IT IS BLAZING HOTLY HE LOWERS IT TO VAL'S POSITION.

QUICKLY VAL LOWERS HIMSELF TO THE WINDOW BELOW AND SWINGS IN

BUT HIS ENEMY HAS PLANNED CAREFULLY—THE WAY TO FREEDOM IS BLOCKED.
— NEXT WEEK—»DESPERATION«.

51

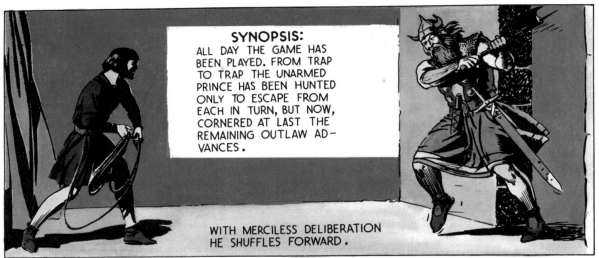

SYNOPSIS: ALL DAY THE GAME HAS BEEN PLAYED. FROM TRAP TO TRAP THE UNARMED PRINCE HAS BEEN HUNTED ONLY TO ESCAPE FROM EACH IN TURN, BUT NOW, CORNERED AT LAST THE REMAINING OUTLAW ADVANCES.

WITH MERCILESS DELIBERATION HE SHUFFLES FORWARD.

VAL ESCAPES THE FIRST SWING OF THE AXE BY A QUICK FLICK OF HIS ROPE.

BUT THE PURSUIT GOES ON FROM ONE LOCKED DOOR TO ANOTHER.

AT LAST THE ROOF WITH THE LAUGHING BRUTE STILL ADVANCING SLOWLY.

THE LAST AVENUE OF ESCAPE IS A NARROW LEDGE, BUT ONE END OF VAL'S ROPE HAS SOMEHOW BECOME ENTANGLED AND HE STRUGGLES TO UNTIE THE OTHER FROM HIS BELT!

52 2-5-38

DEATH CREEPS SLOWLY INCH BY INCH TOWARD THE HELPLESS YOUTH!

SUDDENLY VAL SPRINGS OUT INTO SPACE CARRYING THE OUTLAW WITH HIM -- THE LAST TRICK HAS WORKED!

EVEN AS HIS ENEMY GOES HURTLING TO THE COURTYARD BELOW VAL CRASHES WITH STUNNING FORCE AGAINST THE CASTLE WALL!

—NEXT WEEK
*OUT OF TH[E]
DUNGEONS*

SYNOPSIS: WEARING A HORRIBLE MASK, PRINCE VAL HAS FRIGHTENED ALL THE OUTLAWS FROM THE CASTLE EXCEPT TWO. THESE HARDY RUFFIANS CHASE THE UNARMED PRINCE TO THE ROOF WHERE THEY ARE TRICKED TO THEIR DOOM BY A PIECE OF ROPE.

(1)

AS THE LAST OUTLAW HURTLES TO THE YARD BELOW VAL CRASHES WITH STUNNING FORCE AGAINST THE WALL.

AFTER A TREMENDOUS STRUGGLE THE HALF-CONSCIOUS YOUTH GAINS THE ROOF.

(2)

(3) FINDING AN IRON BAR, VAL SMASHES THE LOCKED DOORS AND ENTERS THE NOW-DESERTED CASTLE.

AFTER A WEARY SEARCH HE DISCOVERS THE KEYS TO THE DUNGEONS.

(4)

53 2-12-38

(5)

AND THE YOUNG PRINCE IS ABLE TO LIBERATE ILENE'S FATHER, THE THANE OF BRANWYN, WHO HAS BEEN IMPRISONED SINCE THE OGRE'S CAPTURE OF THE CASTLE.

(6) THE DUNGEON CELLS ALSO GIVE UP THE REST OF THE THANE'S FAMILY AND RETAINERS.

Hal Foster

VAL'S FIRST THOUGHT IS FOR THE MAID, ILENE, AND HE TELLS THE THANE OF THE HERMITAGE WHERE SHE IS WAITING.

(7)

(8)

THREE DAYS OF HARDSHIP WITH NEITHER FOOD NOR SLEEP HAVE TAKEN THEIR TOLL AND, HIS WORK DONE, THE YOUTHFUL PRINCE COLLAPSES.

(9) THE TENDER HEART OF ILENE BEATS WILDLY WHEN THE MESSENGER ARRIVES WITH THE NEWS OF VAL'S HEROIC DEEDS AND SHE HASTENS TO RETURN.

NEXT WEEK · **CUPID USES AN AXE**

SYNOPSIS: VAL'S STOUT HEART AND NIMBLE WIT HAVE FINALLY RESTORED TO THE THANE OF BRANWYN HIS LANDS AND CASTLE — BUT TO VAL NOTHING IS IMPORTANT SAVE ONLY THAT A MESSENGER HAS GONE TO FETCH THE FAIR ILENE FROM THE HERMITAGE WHERE SHE IS TENDING THE UNLUCKY SIR GAWAIN.

"PRINCE VALIANT HAS SUCCEEDED", OH! ISN'T HE WONDERFUL?" SINGS THE MAID ILENE AS SHE HURRIEDLY BIDS GOOD-BY TO SIR GAWAIN AND THE HERMIT.

VAL REGALES THE THANE WITH THE STORY OF HOW HE TRICKED THE OGRE TO HIS DOOM WITH A GOOSE-SKIN MASK.

BUT ON THE MORROW HIS SOLE OCCUPATION IS GAZING UP THE SUNLIT ROAD BY WHICH ILENE WILL SOON COME RIDING HOMEWARD.

AND THEN SHE COMES, RIDING GAYLY THROUGH THE SPRING WOODS AND VAL'S HEART PLAYS STRANGE TRICKS.

THE OLD THANE AND HIS WIFE WARMLY GREET THE CHILD THEY HAD THOUGHT LOST.

"IN A FEW DAYS SIR GAWAIN WILL BE STRONG ENOUGH TO BE BROUGHT HERE," SAYS ILENE AS THEY WANDER HAPPILY AFIELD.

54 2-19-38

A KINDLY MOON LOOKS DOWN ON AN OLD, OLD STORY THAT A BOY AND GIRL THINK IS NEW.

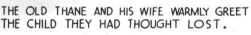

WHILE THE THANE AND HIS LADY GAZE AT A SIGNED PARCHMENT THAT IS TO CAUSE MUCH HEARTBREAK.
—NEXT WEEK—
"THE MARRIAGE CONTRACT"

HAL FOSTER

SYNOPSIS— AFTER WRESTING BRANWYN CASTLE FROM THE OGRE AND RESTORING IT TO THE THANE, VAL BECOMES A PETTED HERO AND HIS CUP OF HAPPINESS IS FILLED TO OVERFLOWING WHEN SWEET ILENE GIVES HIM HER YOUNG HEART. "A POX ON THE WITCH'S DULL PROPHECY THAT I'D KNOW NO CONTENTMENT," LAUGHS VAL HAPPILY.

A CONVEYANCE IS DISPATCHED TO BRING THE WOUNDED SIR GAWAIN TO BRANWYN CASTLE.

NEXT AFTERNOON VAL IS SUMMONED TO THE THANE'S CHAMBER.

"YOU HAVE DONE ME A GREAT SERVICE, PRINCE VALIANT. ASK WHAT YOU WILL OF ME, EVEN TO A THIRD OF MY FIEF."

"I ASK A MORE PRECIOUS REWARD THAN ALL YOUR LANDS, NOBLE SIR, THE HAND OF YOUR DAUGHTER IN MARRIAGE."

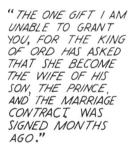

"THE ONE GIFT I AM UNABLE TO GRANT YOU, FOR THE KING OF ORD HAS ASKED THAT SHE BECOME THE WIFE OF HIS SON, THE PRINCE, AND THE MARRIAGE CONTRACT WAS SIGNED MONTHS AGO."

65 2-26-38

"MY BOY," SAYS THE WISE OLD THANE, "SHE WILL BE THE WIFE OF A WEALTHY PRINCE AND SOME DAY A STATELY QUEEN, IN THE SPLENDOR OF COURT LIFE SHE WILL FORGET THIS GIRLISH LOVE FOR A PENNILESS LAD. BESIDES, VAL," SAYS THE THANE LOWERING HIS VOICE, "SHE IS VERY MUCH LIKE HER MOTHER, A FINE WOMAN, BUT ASSERTIVE—— VERY ASSERTIVE."

THE SLEEPLESS BOY, GAZING AT THE WINDOW OF A SLEEPLESS MAID, VOWS — "WHO TAKES ILENE FROM ME MUST FIGHT AND FIGHT HARD."

BUT IN THE CHILL DAWN COMES A MESSENGER CRYING, "SIR GAWAIN IS GONE, CARRIED OFF BY A SORCERESS."

HAL FOSTER

·NEXT WEEK·
THE CHOICE

Prince Valiant

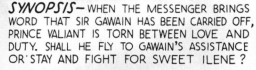

SYNOPSIS – WHEN THE MESSENGER BRINGS WORD THAT SIR GAWAIN HAS BEEN CARRIED OFF, PRINCE VALIANT IS TORN BETWEEN LOVE AND DUTY. SHALL HE FLY TO GAWAIN'S ASSISTANCE OR STAY AND FIGHT FOR SWEET ILENE?

VAL FALTERED BUT AN INSTANT. "*I SHALL RETURN,*" HE CRIES. "*IN SPITE OF YOUR BETROTHAL TO PRINCE ARN I SHALL WIN YOU AND IN SPITE OF THE WITCH'S PROPHECY I SHALL KNOW CONTENTMENT.*"

AND MOUNTING HIS HORSE CLATTERS FROM THE CASTLE

SO FAST DOES HE RIDE THAT ERE SUN-DOWN HE ARRIVES AT THE HERMITAGE.

THE HERMIT TELLS, – "*A GREAT LADY PASSED AND SEEING SIR GAWAIN SLEEPING IN THE SUNLIGHT CAST A SPELL ON HIM AND CARRIED HIM AWAY.*"
"*'TWAS MORGAN LE FEY, HALF-SISTER OF THE KING, BEAUTIFUL, EVIL AND MISTRESS OF STRANGE MAGIC.*"

"*I MUST RIDE TO HER CASTLE DOLOROUS GARDE AND RESCUE SIR GAWAIN.*"

AND AT DAWN SEES FAR OUT IN THE MARSH THE SINISTER CASTLE THAT ALL MEN AVOID.

• NEXT WEEK •
THE SORCERESS

REMOUNTED ON SIR GAWAIN'S GREAT HORSE VAL GALLOPS THROUGH THE NIGHT.

56 3-5-38

SYNOPSIS:
MORGAN LE FEY, BEAUTIFUL AND EVIL – HAS SECRETLY LOVED SIR GAWAIN. FINDING HIM RECOVERING FROM HIS WOUNDS IN A HERMITAGE, SHE CARRIES HIM OFF. VAL COMES TO THE RESCUE! EVEN THOUGH IT COSTS HIM HIS CHANCE OF WINNING THE MAID ILENE.

...ER THE CAUSEWAY THAT EXTENDS TO DOLOROUS GARDE-... OUT IN THE SWAMPS-GALLOPS THE ANXIOUS PRINCE

VAL BLOWS A RESOUNDING BLAST ON THE HORN THAT HANGS BY A CHAIN TO THE CURIOUSLY WROUGHT GATES.

THEY OPEN AND VAL ENTERS THE DREAD CASTLE, SILENTLY ESCORTED BY VERY UN-WHOLESOME–LOOKING ATTENDANTS.

THE LOVELY SORCERESS RECEIVES HIM GRACIOUSLY AND LISTENS TO HIS DEMAND FOR GAWAIN'S FREEDOM.

"YOUR SUSPICIONS WOUND ME, HANDSOME BOY, FOR I HAVE LOVED SIR GAWAIN THESE MANY YEARS AND HAVE ONLY BROUGHT HIM HERE THAT HIS WOUNDS MAY BE TENDERLY TREATED."

THEN SHE ASKS VAL TO TELL HER OF HIS ADVENTURES WITH SIR GAWAIN WHILE A SILENT ATTENDANT SERVES THEM WINE AND SWEET CAKES.

BUT THE WINE CONTAINS A SUBTLE DRUG AND AS HIS STRENGTH EBBS AWAY VAL HEARS A MOCKING LAUGH.

HAL FOSTER.

AND UPON THE HELPLESS YOUTH THE HYPNOTIC SORCERESS CASTS A POWERFUL SPELL.

NEXT WEEK — THE SPELL !

SYNOPSIS—PRINCE VALIANT LEAVES HIS BELOVED ILENE AND HASTENS TO RESCUE SIR GAWAIN FROM THE HANDS OF BEAUTIFUL MORGAN LE FEY, THE SORCERESS, BUT, TRICKED BY A SUBTLE DRUG, HE FALLS UNDER HER EVIL SPELL.

"LITTLE BOYS SHOULD NOT MEDDLE IN THE AFFAIRS OF MORGAN LE FEY."

"YOU SHALL HAVE THE PRIVILEGE OF ASSISTING ME TO WIN A HANDSOME HUSBAND."

"I MUST STILL DECLINE THE HONOR OF MARRYING YOU, FAIR WITCH," SAYS THE COURTEOUS GAWAIN, "FOR 'TIS SAID YOUR HUSBANDS SELDOM OUT-LIVE YOUR FIRST DISPLEASURE."

"WHEN YOUR LITTLE FRIEND SCREAMS IN THE NIGHT YOU MAY CHANGE YOUR MIND."

VAL IS THROWN ROUGHLY INTO A DAMP CELL.

58 3-19-38

UNDER HER EVIL SPELL VAL'S NIGHTS ARE HAUNTED BY TERRIBLE VISIONS.

KNOWING FULL-WELL HIS SCANTY FOOD AND DRINK CONTAINS THE DRUG THAT KEEPS HIM IN HER POWER, HE YET MUST EAT OR STARVE.

A STORM RAGES AND THROUGH THE BARS OF THE HIGH WINDOW VAL HEARS THE SOUND OF WAVES—-AND A PLAN FORMS IN HIS NUMBED BRAIN.

NEXT WEEK—"HOPE"

SYNOPSIS—ENDEAVORING TO RESCUE SIR GAWAIN, VAL FALLS UNDER THE EVIL SPELL OF MORGAN LE FEY, THE SORCERESS. WEAKENED BY A DRUG GIVEN HIM IN HIS WINE, THE YOUNG PRINCE IS UNABLE TO ESCAPE HER WITCHERY.

DURING A STORM VAL HEARS THE SOUND OF WAVES BE-NEATH HIS BARRED WINDOW AND, REMOVING A SHOE—

TIES IT TO A RAVELING FROM HIS GARMENT AND THROWS IT THROUGH THE WINDOW.

"WATER! NOW IF THE DRUG IS GIVEN ME IN THE WINE I MAY YET BE SAVED!"

WITH PLENTY OF WATER TO DRINK HE SPILLS THE DRUGGED WINE ON THE FLOOR AND FEIGNS WEAKNESS.

AS HIS STRENGTH RETURNS HE THROWS OFF THE SPELL AND SETS TO WORK, HIS ONLY TOOL IS A METAL BELT—BUCKLE.

IT IS MANY DAYS BEFORE HE SUCCEEDS IN DISLODG-ING THE STONE THAT HOLDS THE BARS IN PLACE.

ON A STORMY NIGHT HE ESCAPES AND REPLACES THE STONE AND BARS CAREFULLY— HE, TOO, LEAVES MYSTERY BEHIND!

59 3-26-55

THROUGH THE TREACHEROUS SWAMPS HE STRUGGLES TOWARD SHORE.

AND HEADS FOR CAMELOT, THIRTY MILES AWAY.

HAL FOSTER

NEXT WEEK—WISE MERLIN

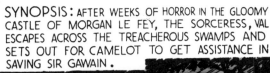

SYNOPSIS: AFTER WEEKS OF HORROR IN THE GLOOMY CASTLE OF MORGAN LE FEY, THE SORCERESS, VAL ESCAPES ACROSS THE TREACHEROUS SWAMPS AND SETS OUT FOR CAMELOT TO GET ASSISTANCE IN SAVING SIR GAWAIN.

HOUR AFTER HOUR VAL TROTS DOGGEDLY ON THROUGH STORM AND DARKNESS.

IN THE EARLY DAWN HE SEES MERLIN'S TOWER IN THE DISTANCE. *"ONE FIGHTS FIRE WITH FIRE; WHY NOT MAGIC WITH MAGIC?"* AND VAL TURNS OFF TOWARD THE CASTLE.

IF ANYONE CAN HELP SIR GAWAIN IT IS WISE MERLIN, THE WIZARD, ADVISER TO KING ARTHUR.

THE WEARY, MUD-STAINED PRINCE IS ADMITTED TO MERLIN'S CHAMBER.

AFTER VAL TELLS HIS STORY, MERLIN SAYS—*"SHE IS EVIL AND WILL MURDER GAWAIN AND CAST HIS BODY IN THE MARSH AT THE APPROACH OF ARMED FORCES. WE MUST BE SUBTLE."*

WHILE VAL RESTS MERLIN SEARCHES THROUGH HIS ANCIENT VOLUMES OF STRANGE LORE.

"I CAN HELP, BUT FIRST YOU MUST SECURE FOR ME SOMETHING THIS SORCERESS HAS WORN, OR HANDLED OR VALUED, THEN I CAN CAST A SPELL."

WELL—ARMED AND MOUNTED, VAL STARTS BACK ON HIS DANGEROUS MISSION —

AND COMES IN SIGHT OF "DOLOROUS GARDE" JUST AS A HUNTING PARTY EMERGES TO GO A-HAWKING
NEXT WEEK— PERILOUS SPORT

SYNOPSIS—TO RESCUE SIR GAWAIN FROM THE CRUEL HANDS OF MORGAN LE FEY, THE SORCERESS, VAL ENLISTS THE AID OF MERLIN, THE MAGICIAN, AND IS COMMANDED BY HIM TO OBTAIN SOME PERSONAL ARTICLE BELONGING TO THE FAIR WITCH.

VAL RETURNS TO "DOLOROUS GARDE" IN TIME TO SEE A HUNTING PARTY LEAVE THE CASTLE.

MORGAN LE FEY AND HER FRIENDS GO A-HAWKING. VAL FOLLOWS AT A DISTANCE.

FROM A PLACE OF CONCEALMENT, VAL SEES LE FEY RELEASE HER FAVORITE FALCON.

THE FALCON PURSUES ITS QUARRY IN VAL'S DIRECTION.

"THAT HAWK IS THE PERSONAL POSSESSION OF MORGAN LE FEY'S THAT I SEEK. HERE GOES!"

FLASHING ACROSS THE MEADOW HE GRASPS THE BIRD BEFORE IT LANDS.

WHEELING ABOUT, VAL SETS SPURS TO HIS MOUNT. WITH A SHOUT OF RAGE THE HUNTERS RACE IN PURSUIT.

REACHING MERLIN TOWER, VAL POUNDS UPON THE DOOR, WHILE THE ANGRY HUNTERS CLOSE IN SWIFTLY

GRIPPING HIS PRIZE TIGHTLY, VAL LASHES OUT WITH HIS SWORD AND, FOR A TIME, HOLDS BACK HIS ATTACKERS.

HAL FOSTER

NEXT WEEK— MERLIN'S CONJURING

61 4-9-38

SYNOPSIS—VAL APPEALS TO MERLIN, THE GREAT MAGICIAN, FOR AID IN RESCUING SIR GAWAIN FROM THE POWER OF MORGAN LE FEY, THE SORCERESS. MERLIN ASKS FOR SOME PERSONAL POSSESSION OF LE FEY'S WITH WHICH TO WORK HIS MAGIC AND VAL STEALS HER PET FALCON, BUT SO SWIFT IS THE PURSUIT THAT HE IS CORNERED AT MERLIN'S GATE.

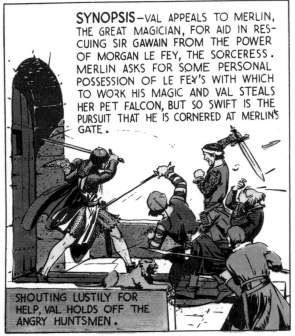

SHOUTING LUSTILY FOR HELP, VAL HOLDS OFF THE ANGRY HUNTSMEN.

HELP COMES UNEXPECTEDLY.

MERLIN APPROVES OF VAL'S SOUVENIR.

MORGAN LE FEY IS FILLED WITH DREAD WHEN SHE HEARS WHO STOLE HER FALCON AND TO WHOM IT WAS TAKEN.

WISE MERLIN SETS TO WORK ON A MAGIC THAT WILL FORCE SIR GAWAIN'S RELEASE.

WHILE VAL WANDERS IN THE GREAT MAGICIAN'S ENCHANTED GARDEN.

BUT EVEN THE STRANGE ILLUSIONS THAT FILL THIS TWILIGHT PLACE CANNOT TURN HIS THOUGHTS FROM FAIR ILENE.

MIDNIGHT; AND INTO THE BEDCHAMBER OF LE FEY THERE COME CRAWLING STRANGE FANTASIES CONJURED UP FROM THE HALF-WORLD BY MERLIN.

NEXT WEEK- SIR GAWAIN IS FREED.

SYNOPSIS— TO FORCE MORGAN LE FEY, THE SORCERESS, TO RELEASE SIR GAWAIN, WHOM SHE IS HOLDING PRISONER, MERLIN CONJURES UP STRANGE TERRORS FROM THE HALF-WORLD OF DREAMS AND MAKES NIGHT HIDEOUS FOR HER.

NO MAGIC THAT SHE CAN DEVISE WILL KEEP BACK THE GHOSTLY HORRORS THAT MAKE HIDEOUS HER EVERY SLEEPING MOMENT.

"NOW GO TO MORGAN LE FEY AND SAY TO HER THAT SHE WILL KNOW NO REST UNTIL YOU AND SIR GAWAIN RETURN HERE SAFELY TO ME."

ARRIVING AT THE GATE OF 'DOLOROUS GARDE' PRINCE VALIANT IS QUIETLY SEIZED—

AND BROUGHT BEFORE THE RAGING SORCERESS AND HER QUEER SERVANTS.

GLADLY WOULD SHE CONDEMN THEM BOTH TO A LINGERING DEATH, BUT VAL REMINDS HER OF MERLIN'S THREAT.

SULLENLY SHE ORDERS SIR GAWAIN'S RELEASE.

"PRICELESS SQUIRE!" LAUGHS THE GRATIFIED GAWAIN, "YOU HAVE SAVED ME FROM PRISON; HAVE SAVED ME FROM DEATH AND NOW, 'S YOU. YOU SAVE ME FROM MATRIMONY!"

"DEAR LADY, YOUR INTEREST IN ME IS MOST FLATTERING, BUT KNOWING THE FATE OF ALL YOUR HUSBANDS, I'D MAKE BUT A NERVOUS BRIDE-GROOM IN THIS UNWHOLESOME PLACE."

63 4-23-38

AS THE LIGHT-HEARTED PAIR DEPART, VAL LEAVES A 'TALISMAN' TO HOLD BACK LE FEY'S STRANGE HENCHMEN.

HAL FOSTER

NEXT WEEK— THE MESSENGER

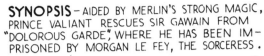

SYNOPSIS—AIDED BY MERLIN'S STRONG MAGIC, PRINCE VALIANT RESCUES SIR GAWAIN FROM "DOLOROUS GARDE", WHERE HE HAS BEEN IM-PRISONED BY MORGAN LE FEY, THE SORCERESS.

THAT HER STRANGE SERVITORS DARE NOT PASS VAL'S CHARM IS EVIDENCE OF THE UNWHOLESOME REGION FROM WHICH SHE HAD RECRUITED THEM.

GAWAIN SINGS HAPPILY IN HIS NEW-FOUND FREEDOM, BUT THE YOUNG PRINCE HURRIES FORWARD ANXIOUSLY.

"YOU ARE UNHAPPY, VAL. IS THERE ANY-THING I CAN DO?" INTO HIS FRIEND'S SYMPATHETIC EAR VAL POURS HIS TALE OF WOE—

—OF HOW ILENE HAS BEEN BETROTHED BY HER FATHER TO PRINCE ARN OF ORD.

"BUT SHE LOVES ONLY ME AND I MEAN TO HAVE HER FOR MY OWN IN SPITE OF HER FATHER, PRINCE ARN OR THE DEVIL, HIMSELF!"

THEY COME AT LAST TO MERLIN'S TOWER.

THE GRATEFUL PAIR THANK THEIR WISE HELPER.

"YOU MAY KEEP THE ARMS I LENT YOU TO USE IN GOOD KING ARTHUR'S SERVICE."

AS THEY NEAR CAMELOT THEY ARE JOINED BY A FELLOW TRAVELER WHO, UNKNOWN TO THEM, BEARS A MESSAGE THAT WILL CHANGE VAL'S WHOLE LIFE.

NEXT WEEK— WEDDING INVITATIONS

SYNOPSIS:- GAWAIN, THE LIGHT HEARTED, AND
PRINCE VALIANT, HIS NIMBLE SQUIRE, HASTEN
TO CAMELOT TO REPORT THE SUCCESS OF THEIR
LATEST QUEST. EACH MINUTE SPENT AWAY FROM
SWEET ILENE IS, TO VAL, A WEARY YEAR AND
HE SPURS FORWARD SWIFTLY.

AT A CROSSROAD THEY ARE JOINED BY A
KNIGHT, WHO, UNKNOWN TO THEM, BEARS
A FATEFUL MESSAGE.

THE KNIGHTS OF THE ROUND TABLE WELCOME
THEM BOISTEROUSLY, FOR THE MERRY GAWAIN
AND HIS WITTY SQUIRE ARE GREAT FAVORITES.

A FEAST IS HELD IN THEIR HONOR.

KING ARTHUR RISES TO ANNOUNCE THAT A
JOYOUS MESSAGE IS TO BE READ.

65 5-7-38

THE KNIGHT THEY
HAD MET RIDING INTO CAMELOT
ARISES AND READS-"*THE KING OF
ORD INVITES YOU ONE AND ALL TO A GREAT
TOURNAMENT TO CELEBRATE THE MARRIAGE OF
HIS SON, PRINCE ARN, TO ILENE OF BRANWYN.*"

IT IS A TERRIBLE BLOW TO VAL AND HIS HEART
IS SICK WITH RAGE AND SORROW.

HIDES HIS BREAKING HEART AND THAT NIGHT NO
ONE IS GAYER THAN THIS BRAVE AND MANLY PRINCE.

BUT WHEN THE LIGHTS GO OUT ONE BY ONE
AND ALL IS SILENT IN THE GREAT CASTLE,
IT IS ONLY A HURT BOY WHO QUIETLY SOBS
OUT HIS HEARTBREAK IN THE DARK.

GAWAIN COVERS THE SLEEPING LAD
WITH HIS SCARLET CLOAK.
NEXT WEEK—THE DISAPPEARANCE

SYNOPSIS— WHILE THE FEAST IS AT ITS HEIGHT A MESSENGER PROCLAIMS THAT THE MARRIAGE OF PRINCE ARN TO THE GOLDEN-HAIRED ILENE WILL TAKE PLACE THE FOLLOWING WEEK. NO ONE BUT GAWAIN KNOWS HOW MUCH VAL LOVES THIS SLIM MAID. IN THE MORNING VAL HAS DISAPPEARED!

SIR GAWAIN SEARCHES ALL CAMELOT FOR HIS YOUNG FRIEND, BUT NOWHERE CAN HE BE FOUND.

FOR WITH THE DAWN'S LIGHT HAD COME RESOLUTION. VAL HAD DETERMINED TO SEEK PRINCE ARN AND FIGHT HIM FOR FAIR ILENE!

WELL-ARMED, VAL DEPARTS FROM CAMELOT IN THE EARLY MORN.

ANXIOUS TO FIND PRINCE ARN BEFORE THE WEDDING CAN TAKE PLACE, VAL RAGES IMPATIENTLY WHEN HIS PATH IS BLOCKED BY A QUESTING KNIGHT.

IN ACCORDANCE WITH CUSTOM, THE KNIGHT CHALLENGES TO A TILT — VAL SETS SHIELD AND LANCE AND —

HIS ANGER FLAMING AT THE DELAY, CHARGES WITH DEADLY FURY.

VAL GALLOPS FORWARD, NOT EVEN PAUSING TO INQUIRE THE NAME OF THE KNIGHT WHO LIES BRUISED, DAZED AND WONDERING IF BY CHANCE LIGHTNING HAD STRUCK.

RIDING TOWARD THE KINGDOM OF ORD, VAL FINDS AMPLE EVIDENCE THAT VIKING RAIDERS ARE AGAIN LAYING WASTE THE COASTS OF ENGLAND.

HAL FOSTER

VAL, GIVING NO HEED TO THE PRESENCE OF DANGE ENTERS TOWARD A NARROW BRIDGE.

NEXT WEEK— *PRINCE ARN*

66 5-15-38

Prince Valiant

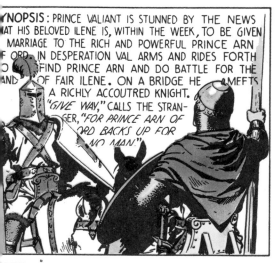

SYNOPSIS: PRINCE VALIANT IS STUNNED BY THE NEWS THAT HIS BELOVED ILENE IS, WITHIN THE WEEK, TO BE GIVEN IN MARRIAGE TO THE RICH AND POWERFUL PRINCE ARN OF ORD. IN DESPERATION VAL ARMS AND RIDES FORTH TO FIND PRINCE ARN AND DO BATTLE FOR THE HAND OF FAIR ILENE. ON A BRIDGE HE MEETS A RICHLY ACCOUTRED KNIGHT.
"GIVE WAY," CALLS THE STRANGER, "FOR PRINCE ARN OF ORD BACKS UP FOR NO MAN."

"PRINCE ARN, IS IT?" CRIES VAL, "WELL, THERE MUST ALWAYS BE A FIRST TIME.—PREPARE TO FIGHT, FOR BUT ONE OF US WILL CROSS THIS BRIDGE!"

COUCHING THEIR LANCES THEY CHARGE SWIFTLY ONTO THE FRAIL BRIDGE—

AND MEET WITH SO GREAT A CRASH THAT THE BRIDGE RAIL GIVES WAY—

AND ARN TOPPLES INTO THE SWIRLING WATERS WITH A MIGHTY SPLASH.

ENCUMBERED BY HIS HEAVY ARMOR HE IS WASHED INTO THE POOL BELOW AND SINKS FROM SIGHT. VAL DOES NOT HESITATE—

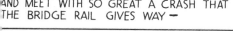

BUT CASTING ASIDE SWORD, SHIELD AND HELMET, PLUNGES AFTER.

67 5-22-38

IN THE GREEN DEPTHS OF THE POOL VAL FINDS PRINCE ARN AND STRUGGLES SHORE-WARD WITH HIS BURDEN.

AND SOON REVIVES HIS EXHAUSTED RIVAL.

"WHY DID YOU TROUBLE TO SAVE ME WHEN FORTUNE SEEMED TO FAVOR YOUR CAUSE?" "IF YOU ARE TO DIE THIS DAY, IT WILL BE BY MY HAND IN FAIR FIGHT!"

"FOR TWO OF US CANNOT MARRY MISTRESS ILENE.—I MEAN TO, OR DIE."

HALF THEIR WEAPONS BEING LOST, THEY AGREE TO FARE FORTH TOGETHER UNTIL SUFFICIENTLY ARMED FOR THEIR DUEL.

NEXT WEEK—THE DUEL

HAL FOSTER

Prince Valiant

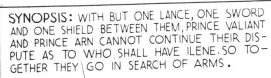

IN THE DAYS OF KING ARTHUR BY HAROLD R FOSTER

SYNOPSIS: WITH BUT ONE LANCE, ONE SWORD AND ONE SHIELD BETWEEN THEM, PRINCE VALIANT AND PRINCE ARN CANNOT CONTINUE THEIR DISPUTE AS TO WHO SHALL HAVE ILENE. SO TOGETHER THEY GO IN SEARCH OF ARMS.

"WE SHALL RIDE TOWARD BRANWYN TOGETHER BUT ONLY ONE OF US WILL FINISH THE JOURNEY."

"WE WILL BORROW WHAT WE NEED FROM YONDER BLACK KNIGHT."

"YOU MAY HELP YOURSELVES TO ANYTHING OF MINE YOU NEED IF EITHER OF YOU BE MAN ENOUGH TO TAKE IT"

ARN WINS THE TOSS OF A COIN AND, TAKING VAL'S LANCE AND SHIELD, ADDRESSES THE STRANGER.

A THUNDERING OF HOOFS, A MIGHTY SHOCK AND THE BLACK KNIGHT GOES DOWN WITH A CRASH!

CALMLY THE TWO METTLESOME LADS ARM THEMSELVES AND PREPARE TO WIN EITHER ILENE OR DEATH

"ILENE OR DEATH!" SHOUTS VAL. "DEATH OR ILENE!" CRIES ARN, AS THEY MEET FURIOUSLY.

THE STRUGGLE RAGES WHILE THE SUN DESCENDS HALF-WAY DOWN THE EVENING SKY AND STILL THE WEARY AND BLEEDING LADS FIGHT DOGGEDLY ON. 68 5-29-38

HAL FOSTER

A SHOUT FROM THE BLACK KNIGHT MAKES THEM PAUSE AND THERE, AT THE EDGE OF THE GLADE, IS A PARTY OF VIKING RAIDERS.

NEXT WEEK—ILENE ABDUCTED!

Prince Valiant
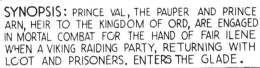

SYNOPSIS: PRINCE VAL, THE PAUPER AND PRINCE ARN, HEIR TO THE KINGDOM OF ORD, ARE ENGAGED IN MORTAL COMBAT FOR THE HAND OF FAIR ILENE WHEN A VIKING RAIDING PARTY, RETURNING WITH LOOT AND PRISONERS, ENTERS THE GLADE.

"TO HORSE," SHOUTS THE BLACK KNIGHT, "TO HORSE AND LET'S HAVE AT THEM!"

MOUNTING SWIFTLY, THEY SPUR THEIR GREAT WAR-HORSES INTO THE BAND OF BARBARIANS, SLASHING MIGHTILY RIGHT AND LEFT UNTIL THE VIKINGS BREAK AND FLEE WILDLY, LEAVING THEIR PRISONERS BEHIND.

"PRINCE VAL, FOR HEAVEN'S SAKE HELP US. WE WERE ESCORTING MISTRESS ILENE TO THE PALACE OF THE KING OF ORD WHEN WE WERE CAPTURED BY THE VIKINGS — THEY ARE TAKING HER TO THE COAST!"

"MOUNT, SIR KNIGHT, AND CARRY THIS NEWS TO GOOD KING ARTHUR AT CAMELOT —RIDE!"

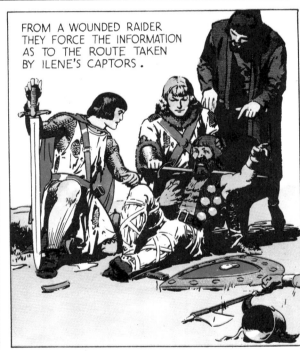

FROM A WOUNDED RAIDER THEY FORCE THE INFORMATION AS TO THE ROUTE TAKEN BY ILENE'S CAPTORS.

SIDE BY SIDE THE TWO YOUNG PRINCES SPUR FORWARD ON THEIR DANGEROUS MISSION, THEIR QUARREL FORGOTTEN IN THE FACE OF ILENE'S PERIL.

AT THE BRIDGE OVER DUNDORN GLEN THEY REST AND AWAIT THE COMING OF THE RAIDERS WITH THEIR FAIR CAPTIVE.

NEXT MORNING THE RISING SUN DISCLOSES NOT ONE PARTY OF VIKINGS, BUT TWO, AND THE BRAVE LADS ARE CAUGHT BETWEEN—

NEXT WEEK— **THE SINGING SWORD!**

SYNOPSIS: AT DUNDORN GLEN, PRINCE VALIANT AND HIS RIVAL, STALWART PRINCE ARN, AWAIT THE BAND OF VIKING RAIDERS WHO HAVE STOLEN ILENE. AT DAWN TWO BANDS OF VIKINGS APPEAR FROM OPPOSITE DIRECTIONS AND THE BRAVE LADS ARE HEMMED IN AT THE BRIDGE.

BUT ILENE IS WITH NEITHER BAND, SO THEY MUST CUT THEIR WAY THROUGH AND CONTINUE THEIR SEARCH.

"LET'S WAIT UNTIL THAT BAND IS ON THE NARROW BRIDGE, THEN A CHARGE BETWEEN THE MOUNTED MEN WILL CAUSE GREAT CONFUSION AND MAYBE WE WILL WIN THROUGH."

"NOW BRAVE ENEMY," SHOUTS ARN, "STRIKE HARD AND TRUE FOR ENGLAND AND FAIR ILENE!"

"FOR ILENE!" RINGS THEIR BATTLE CRY AS THEY THUNDER ACROSS THE BRIDGE AND CRASH HEADLONG INTO THE CLOSE-PACKED RAIDERS!

VAL'S STRATEGY WINS THROUGH, BUT HIS HORSE, RECEIVING A MORTAL WOUND, STUMBLES AND FALLS

"GO, ARN," SAYS VAL, "THE FATE OF ILENE IS NOW IN YOUR HANDS—PURSUIT WILL BE DELAYED HERE AS LONG AS I CAN WIELD A SWORD."

ARN DRAWS HIS GREAT SWORD. "TAKE THIS, VAL, IT IS THE FAMOUS "SINGING SWORD" AND BEARS A CHARM. ONLY BY MIRACLES CAN YOU OUTLIVE THE NEXT HOUR."

70 6-12-38

HAL FOSTER

·NEXT WEEK
THE SONG
OF THE
SWORD

AND ALONG THE KEEN EDGE OF THE "SINGING SWORD" THE WIND HUMS GLEEFULLY AS VAL STRIDES OUT ONTO THE BRIDGE TO FACE FIFTY ENRAGED VIKINGS!

Prince Valiant

SYNOPSIS: GLADLY WOULD PRINCE ARN HAVE STAYED TO DIE, FIGHTING SIDE BY SIDE WITH VAL, BUT THIS IS NO TIME FOR HEROIC GESTURES. ILENE IS STILL HELD BY THE VIKING RAIDERS. ARN SPURS ONWARD AND VAL PREPARES TO HOLD BACK THE PURSUIT.

"I WISH THE GODS HAD MADE YONDER BRAVE FOOL MY FRIEND INSTEAD OF MY SWORN ENEMY."

THE JEWELLED HILT OF THE "SINGING SWORD" FITS SNUGLY IN HIS HAND, AS VAL MARCHES RESOLUTELY TO HIS FATE.

THE NORTHMEN ARE BEWILDERED AT SUCH FOOLHARDY COURAGE, SUSPECTING A TRICK— BUT ONE HUGE VIKING—

A CAPTAIN, STEPS FORWARD SAYING, "MY TWO-EDGED AXE WILL SOLVE THIS RIDDLE"— VAL'S BLADE SWISHES SOFTLY, WAITING—

BUT ERE THE AXE CAN FALL, THE "SING-ING SWORD" SHRIEKS EXULTANTLY, AS THE KEEN EDGE BITES THROUGH SHIELD AND HELMET AND A WARRIOR'S SOUL GOES WINGING TO VALHALLA.

"COME CLOSER," TAUNTS VAL, "MY BEAUTIFUL SWORD IS THIRSTY," AND HALF A HUNDRED HARDY VIKINGS CROWD FORWARD.

AGAIN AND AGAIN THE TERRIBLE SWORD RISES AND FALLS, GLEAM-ING WET IN THE SUNLIGHT, AND ABOVE THE ROAR OF THE WATERS AND THE CLASHING OF ARMS CAN BE HEARD VAL'S RING-ING BATTLE-CRY, "FOR ILENE."

= NEXT WEEK =
THE EXECUTIONER

HAL FOSTER

71 6-19-38

SYNOPSIS: PRINCE ARN RIDES ON TO FREE THEIR BELOVED ILENE FROM THE HANDS OF RAIDERS, WHILE VAL, HIS HORSE KILLED, STANDS ALONE ON THE BRIDGE AT DUNDORN GLEN TO DELAY PURSUIT — ONE AGAINST FIFTY!

WITH RAGE IN HIS HEART AND THE TERRIBLE "SINGING SWORD" IN HIS HAND, VAL WRITES HIS NAME LARGE IN THE MEMORIES OF HIS FOES.

AT LAST THEY DRAW BACK IN AMAZEMENT AT THIS TIRELESS YOUTH WITH THE NIMBLE SWORD THAT HISSES THROUGH CHAIN AND LEATHER AND IRON.

BUT WEAKENED BY A SCORE OF WOUNDS, VAL SINKS SLOWLY TO THE GROUND, STILL FACING HIS ENEMIES.

"SURELY, THIS CAN BE NO LESS THAN A KING'S SON, CARRY HIM TO OUR CHIEF TO BE RANSOMED."

WHEN VAL NEXT OPENS HIS EYES HE IS BEING BORNE TO THE COAST ON THE WARRIORS' SPEARS — WELL, HIS WORK IS DONE; ARN HAS ESCAPED TO FIND ILENE.

BESIDE HIS TWO SHIPS SITS THAGNAR, THE SEA ROVER, AWAITING THE RETURN OF HIS RAIDERS. WHEN VAL IS BROUGHT BEFORE HIM HE ROARS, "I TOLD YOU MEN NOT TO ANNOY ME WITH PRISONERS."

"KILL HIM," ORDERS THAGNAR. HE SPOKE THE SAME LANGUAGE AS VAL'S FATHER, THE EXILED KING.

72 6-26-38

"NOW, IF I WISHED TO KILL A MAN I'D DO IT MYSELF," MOCKS VAL, "BUT PERHAPS BOLD THAGNAR PREFERS TO REST IN THE SHADE LIKE AN OLD WOMAN AND HAS NO TASTE FOR DANGER."

"THE BANTAM COCK CROWS LOUD.—YES, THAGNAR WILL REST IN THE SHADE WHILE YOU MAKE GOOD YOUR BOAST AGAINST MY EXECUTIONER WHO SITS YONDER, WHETTING HIS DEADLY BLADE."

HAL FOSTER

NEXT WEEK—"A PLEA FOR MERCY."

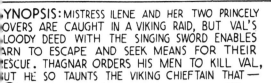

SYNOPSIS: MISTRESS ILENE AND HER TWO PRINCELY LOVERS ARE CAUGHT IN A VIKING RAID, BUT VAL'S BLOODY DEED WITH THE SINGING SWORD ENABLES ARN TO ESCAPE AND SEEK MEANS FOR THEIR RESCUE. THAGNAR ORDERS HIS MEN TO KILL VAL, BUT HE SO TAUNTS THE VIKING CHIEFTAIN THAT—

"SO—OUR LITTLE ROOSTER STILL WANTS TO FIGHT, EH? THEN HE MAY AMUSE US BY DANCING WITH OUR EXECUTIONER."

DROOPING WITH WEARINESS AND WEAKENED BY A SCORE OF WOUNDS, VAL FACES HIS TREMENDOUS OPPONENT.

THE MIGHTY EXECUTIONER TOYS WITH HIM SAYING, "I SHALL INFLICT A THOUSAND SMALL WOUNDS UNTIL YOU HOWL FOR MERCY."

"NAY," SAYS VAL LOUD ENOUGH FOR ALL TO HEAR, "FOR I SEE BY THE STUPIDITY ON YOUR DULL FACE THAT YOU WILL FALL A VICTIM—

TO ANY SIMPLE TRICK AND WILL HOWL TO ME FOR MERCY—

WHEN YOUR BONES CRACKLE LIKE DRY TWIGS!"

CLAMPING A TERRIBLE GRIP ON THE BEWILDERED GIANT, VAL EXERTS ALL HIS REMAINING STRENGTH—

TURNS HIS BELLOWING VICTIM OVER AND PINS HIM HELPLESSLY.

73 7-3-38

HAL FOSTER

"SHALL I LEAN FORWARD AND MAIM YOUR EXECUTIONER, THAGNAR, OR ARE YOU SATISFIED?"

NEXT WEEK—ILENE !

73

SYNOPSIS: VAL, A PRISONER OF THE VIKINGS, IS CONDEMNED TO DEATH, BUT HE TRICKS THAGNAR INTO LETTING HIM DIE FIGHTING AND THEN TRICKS HIS HUGE OPPONENT INTO HELPLESSNESS.

"WHAT DOES THAGNAR SAY NOW?" "ENOUGH,— YOU HAVE WELL-EARNED YOUR FREEDOM—YOU MAY GO."

"IT IS NOT FREE-DOM FOR MYSELF I DESIRE, BUT FOR ANOTHER WHOM YOUR RAIDERS HAVE TAKEN—"

"YONDER MAID, ILENE OF BRANWYN, FOR WHOM I HAVE BEEN SEARCHING."

FOR VAL'S QUICK EYE HAD SEEN A BAND OF RETURNING RAIDERS WITH GOLDEN-HAIRED ILENE AMONG THEIR LOOT.

"WHAT," ROARS THAGNAR, "WAS IT FOR THIS THIN WENCH YOU RISKED YOUR LIFE, KILLED MY MEN AND RUINED MY EXECUTIONER?"

BUT VAL HAS ALREADY FOR-GOTTEN SUCH TRIVIAL TROUBLES AS THAGNAR AND HIS VIKINGS IN THE JOY OF SEEING ILENE AGAIN.

"HAVE COURAGE; ARN IS FREE AND WILL, SOMEHOW, CONTRIVE OUR RESCUE — AND YOU ARE LOVELIER THAN EVER !"

74 7-10-38

"I MUST HAVE THIS LAD, HE HAS WIT AND DARING, COURAGE AND SKILL. HE WILL CAPTAIN ONE OF MY SHIPS AND BE-COME A GREAT SEA-ROVER."

THE TWO DESPERATE YOUNG LOVERS ARE PLACED UNDER GUARD UNTIL THE SHIPS ARE MADE READY.

THAGNAR MUST HAVE COME FROM THE EAST WHERE ONCE VAL'S FATHER HAD RULED, FOR HE SPEAKS THE SAME TONGUE — VAL SCRATCHES A MESSAGE ON A ROCK.

HAL FOSTER

FOR VAL KNOWS THAT PRINCE ARN WILL NEVER FALTER IN A QUEST ONCE UNDERTAKEN AND, SOONER OR LATER, WILL FIND HIS MESSAGE — NOR IS HE WRONG !

ILENE — OR EAST TO JUTES LAND VAL

NEXT WEEK: THE PURSUIT

SYNOPSIS: VAL AND PRINCE ARN ARE BATTLING FOR THE HAND OF ILENE WHEN ALL THREE ARE CAUGHT IN A VIKING RAID. VAL'S GOOD USE OF THE SINGING SWORD ALLOWS ARN TO ESCAPE AND HE SEARCHES FRANTICALLY FOR ILENE.

FOLLOWING THE RAIDERS TO THE COAST, HE ARRIVES TOO LATE AND FINDS ONLY VAL'S MESSAGE SCRATCHED ON A STONE.

CASTING ASIDE HIS HEAVY ARMOR, ARN RACES MADLY TO HIS FATHER'S PALACE AT ORD.

AFTER BITTER ARGUING THE KING AT LAST CONSENTS TO FURNISH A SHIP AND MEN FOR THE PURSUIT.

A PICKED COMPANY OF SAILORS AND ADVENTUROUS YOUNG KNIGHTS AWAIT IMPATIENTLY THE INCOMING TIDE.

75 7-17-38

WISHING TO WIN VAL OVER TO HIS BAND, THAGNAR SHOWS HIS PRISONERS EVERY COURTESY—WHILE HE LOVINGLY HOLDS THE BEAUTIFUL, DEADLY SINGING SWORD.

"BE CALM, ILENE—FAR ASTERN I SEE A PURSUING SAIL. BRAVE ARN IS COMING."

TO GIVE ARN TIME TO APPROACH UNSEEN THEY DIRECT ATTENTION FORWARD.

WITH EVERY CLOTH BENT TO THE BREEZE, EVEN TO THEIR CLOAKS; WITH PRINCE AND NOBLES STRAINING AT THE OARS BESIDE THE SAILORS; ARN'S SHIP COMES FOAMING ACROSS THE SUNLIT WATER.

NEXT WEEK—A SIREN SONG

SYNOPSIS: SATISFIED WITH HIS LOOT AND PRISONERS, THAGNAR SETS SAIL FOR HOME. VAL AND ILENE, GAZING LONGINGLY AT THE FADING SHORES OF ENGLAND, SEE A PURSUING SAIL ON THE FAR HORIZON.

IT IS PRINCE ARN IN SWIFT PURSUIT, SAILS SET AND EVERY MAN STRAINING AT THE OARS.

ARN'S SHIP GAINS RAPIDLY AND IS SOON IN PLAIN SIGHT — IF ONLY VAL CAN HOLD THE SEA-ROVERS' ATTENTION UNTIL ARN IS WITHIN STRIKING DISTANCE!

SEIZING A LYRE FROM AMONG THE PILE OF LOOT, VAL RUNS FORWARD AND LEAPS INTO THE SHROUDS.

LIFTING HIS CLEAR VOICE IN A WILD, HAUNTING MELODY, HE SINGS OF HIS HOME IN THE LONELY MARSHES WHERE THE SEA-WIND FOREVER WHISPERS AN ANCIENT SONG AMONG THE SWAYING REEDS. THE FIERCE SEA-ROVERS RELAX AND DREAM OF THEIR LITTLE HOMES BESIDE THE RESTLESS SEA.

AND CLOSER AND YET CLOSER GLIDES ARN'S SHIP, UNNOTICED UNTIL THE BEAT OF THE OARS CAN BE PLAINLY HEARD.

THEN THE PIRATES AWAKE WITH A START AND ORDERS ARE SHOUTED BY THE ANGRY THAGNAR.

THE SECOND SHIP SHORTENS SAIL AND TURNS TO INTERCEPT THE DARING PURSUERS.

NEXT WEEK—**THE SEA FIGHT**

SYNOPSIS: VAL HOLDS THE SEA-ROVER'S ATTENTION UNTIL PRINCE ARN'S RESCUE SHIP IS ALMOST UPON THEM. ONE OF THE TWO PIRATE SHIPS TURNS TO INTERCEPT.

THE SEA-ROVER SHORTENS SAIL AND PREPARES FOR BATTLE.

SWINGING WIDE MOMENTARILY ARN SUDDENLY TURNS AND BEARS DOWN ON HIS ENEMY.

DRIVEN BY SAIL AND OAR ENGLISH OAK MEETS DANISH CEDAR WITH A TEARING CRASH.

BUT A SEA FIGHT IS THE BREATH OF LIFE TO THESE HARDY ROVERS AND THEY SWARM UPON ARN'S SHIP.

AND THAGNAR SAILS CALMLY ON WITH ALL THE TREASURES FROM HIS RAIDS — THERE WILL NOW BE LESS TO DIVIDE IT AMONG.

VAL IS DESPERATE! STRIKING THAGNAR A STAGGERING BLOW HE TEARS THE "SINGING SWORD" FROM HIS GRASP —

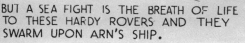

SPEEDS TO THE MAST AND BRINGS THE GREAT SAIL CRASHING DOWN AMONG THE ASTONISHED VIKINGS.

AVOIDING HIS PURSUERS, HE RUNS NIMBLY AFT ON THE GUNWALE —

77 7-31-38

STRIKES DOWN THE HELMSMAN AND, BEFORE ANYONE CAN REACH HIM, CRIPPLES THE STEERING SWEEP.

HAL FOSTER

NEXT WEEK—ILENE ALONE

SYNOPSIS: THAGNAR SAILS CALMLY ON WITH THE PLUNDER AND HIS TWO PRISONERS, WHILE PRINCE ARN'S RESCUE SHIP IS DELAYED BY THE SECOND SEA-ROVER. IN DESPERATION VAL SEIZES THE "SINGING-SWORD," CUTS LOOSE THE SAIL AND DESTROYS THE RUDDER.

WITHOUT SHIELD OR ARMOR VAL STANDS FACING CERTAIN DEATH AT THE HANDS OF THE ENRAGED PIRATES.

"SWIM TO PRINCE ARN'S VESSEL AND HELP HIM SAVE ME—YOUR DEATH HERE COULD HELP NO ONE."

PICKING UP A LEATHERN BUCKET VAL LEAPS INTO THE SEA—

AND DISAPPEARS BENEATH THE WATER. ONLY THE BUCKET CAN BE SEEN BOBBING ON THE WAVES.

BUT VAL IS USING THE BUCKET BOTH TO HIDE IN AND TO HELP REMAIN AFLOAT DESPITE THE WEIGHT OF HIS GREAT SWORD.

SWIMMING AROUND TO THE STERN OF ARN'S SHIP, VAL CLAMBERS UP THE STEERING OAR

78 8-7-38

AND ARMS HIMSELF HURRIEDLY.

PRINCE ARN AND HIS KNIGHTS ARE BATTLING DESPERATELY WHEN A FAMILIAR BATTLE-CRY RINGS OUT "FOR ILENE!"

"IT'S VAL," CRIES ARN AND SIDE BY SIDE THEY THROW THEMSELVES FIERCELY FORWARD UNTIL THE LAST PIRATE IS HURLED INTO THE SEA.

HAL FOSTER

VICTORY, YES, BUT HAS ALLOWED THAGN TIME TO REPAIR HI SHIP AND CARRY ILENE TO THE FA HORIZON.

NEXT WEEK— LOST!

SYNOPSIS: THE ARRIVAL OF PRINCE VALIANT TURNS THE TIDE OF BATTLE AND THE PIRATES ARE SWEPT FROM ARN'S RESCUE SHIP INTO THE SEA, BUT THAGNAR HAS REPAIRED THE DAMAGE DONE HIS SHIP AND HAS SAILED AWAY WITH ILENE.

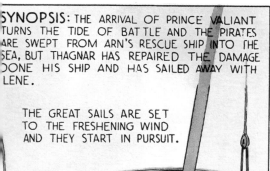

THE GREAT SAILS ARE SET TO THE FRESHENING WIND AND THEY START IN PURSUIT.

AT SUNSET THE WIND HAS BECOME A HOWLING GALE, BUT STILL ARN HOLDS HIS COURSE.

WHEN THE FULL FORCE OF THE STORM BURSTS UPON THEM, THEY WORK LIKE MAD TO KEEP THE CRAFT AFLOAT.

THROUGH THE NIGHT THEY RIDE THE MOUNTAINOUS WAVES AT A SEA-ANCHOR.

AT DAWN THERE IS NO SIGN OF THAGNAR'S SHIP IN ALL THAT EMPTY WASTE OF ANGRY SEA.

— THEN BEGINS THE LONG, WEARY SEARCH FOR SOME NEWS OF THAGNAR—FROM THE GRIM FIÖRDS OF THE NORTH TO THE SALT MARSHES IN THE SOUTH.

WEARIED FROM ALMOST CONSTANT FIGHTING THE TATTERED SURVIVORS AT LAST CALL A HALT.

"GALLANT COMPANIONS, THE SEARCH BY SEA IS FRUITLESS, SO VAL AND I WILL CONTINUE ON LAND, ALONE. GOOD-BYE AND GOOD LUCK."

79 8-14-38

HAL FOSTER

THE SHIP DEPARTS AND THE TWO RIVALS FACE A STRANGE CONTINENT ALONE.

NEXT WEEK — THE SEARCH

SYNOPSIS: DAY AFTER DAY THEY SEARCH THE EMPTY SEA FOR THAGNAR'S SHIP—THE SHIP THAT CARRIED AWAY LOVELY ILENE. DISMISSING THEIR OWN VESSEL, ARN AND VAL SET OUT BY LAND, TO SEEK THAGNAR'S VILLAGE.

THE YOUNG PRINCES BID FAREWELL TO THE LAST LINK WITH THEIR HOMELAND.

ACROSS WEARY MILES OF SHIFTING SANDS THEY MARCH SIDE BY SIDE.

AT EVERY HUT AND VILLAGE THEY INQUIRE OF THAGNAR'S WHEREABOUTS, ALWAYS IN DANGER.

WEEK AFTER WEEK IN SUN AND STORM, NEVER FALTERING, ACROSS THE GREAT SALT MARSHES—

AND IN THE DEPTHS OF GREAT FORESTS THEY SEARCH FOR SOME HINT THAT WILL LEAD THEM TO ILENE.

DESPITE THEIR HARDSHIPS AND DANGER THEY PRACTISE THE RULES OF COURTESY AND FORTITUDE LAID DOWN BY THEIR WISE KING ARTHUR—

AND EACH DAY SET ASIDE AN HOUR TO BETTER THEMSELVES AT SWORD PLAY.

AT LAST THEY MEET SOME FISHERMEN WHO SPEAK THE SAME LANGUAGE AS THAGNAR DOES. THEY ADVISE THE BOYS TO SEEK THAGNAR'S KING FOR INFORMATION.

"KING SLIGON OF THULE! THE TYRANT WHO STOLE MY FATHER'S THRONE AND I MUST BEG HIM FOR A FAVOR!" SAYS VAL BITTERLY. "OR BE MURDERED IF YOU ARE RECOGNIZED," ADDS ARN.

TURNING INLAND AS DIRECTED, THEY AT LAST COME IN SIGHT OF THE KING'S CASTLE.

"ONCE MY FATHER DEALT JUSTICE IN YONDER CASTLE WHERE NOW A TYRANT RULES AND WEEDS GROW IN THE GARDENS WHERE I PLAYED IN CHILDHOOD."

80 8-21-38

AND AGAIN PRINCE VALIANT ENTERS THE FAMILIAR PORTALS THAT HE ONCE CALLED HOME

NEXT WEEK— **THE TYRANT**

SYNOPSIS: HAGNAR, SEA [R]OVER FOR KING [R]IGON, HAS SAILED [A]WAY WITH LOVELY [IL]ENE. TO FIND HIM [A]RN AND VAL GO [TO] THE KING EVEN [TH]OUGH HE IS THE [T]YRANT WHO [ST]OLE THE THRONE [F]ROM VAL'S [FA]THER.

SAYS THE WILY OLD CHAMBERLAIN TO THE KING, "YOUR OLD ENEMY ESCAPED TO ENGLAND. HE HAD A SON,—THIS LAD FROM ENGLAND SPEAKS OUR TONGUE AND LOOKS LIKE—"

"BY THUNDER, YES! MY CROWN IS NOT SAFE AS LONG AS ONE OF THAT DEVIL'S BREED LIVES—HANG HIM!"

PRINCE ARN SPEAKS, QUIETLY—"OH! FOOLISH KING, WHY SOIL YOUR HANDS WITH UNNECESSARY MURDER? WE SEEK ILENE, BESIDE WHOSE BEAUTY YOUR KINGDOM IS A PALTRY THING—HER CROWN OF GOLDEN HAIR IS MORE PRECIOUS THAN THAT UNEASY BAUBLE THAT SETS SO HEAVILY ON YOUR HEAD—WE HAVE SEEN ILENE LAUGHING IN THE SUNLIGHT AND WE HAVE SEEN YOUR KINGDOM—YOUR KINGDOM IS SAFE."

[OH! STOP YOUR HIGH-] [SO]UNDING NONSENSE [A]ND GO, BOTH OF YOU, [G]ET OUT BEFORE YOU [T]ALK ME TO DEATH."

81 8-28-38

"THE FOOLS," MUTTERS THE LONELY TYRANT, "THE GLORIOUS HIGH-HEARTED FOOLS. WHAT A DRAB AND FUTILE THING IS MY KINGDOM BESIDE THE SPLENDOR OF THEIR YOUTH."

SIDE BY SIDE THEY STRIDE FROM THE CASTLE, ONCE AGAIN ON THEIR UNENDING SEARCH— BUT—

NEXT WEEK—"NEWS AT LAST"

SYNOPSIS: IN THEIR SEARCH FOR THE LOST ILENE, ARN AND VAL GO TO KING SLIGON OF THULE, WHOSE SEA ROVER, THAGNAR, HAD CARRIED HER AWAY. THEY BARELY ESCAPE WITH THEIR LIVES.

ERE THEY LEAVE THE PALACE A MESSENGER HALTS THEM.

"THE KING BIDS YOU TAKE YONDER BOAT AND GO TO THE MOUTH OF THE RIVER, WHERE YOU WILL FIND THAGNAR'S VILLAGE."

SWIFTLY THEY GLIDE DOWNSTREAM FOLLOWING THEIR FIRST REAL CLUE.

THE VILLAGERS TELL THEM:—"*THAGNAR NEVER RETURNED FROM HIS RAID ON THE ENGLISH COAST.*"

WITH DESPAIR IN THEIR HEARTS THEY SEARCH THE SHORE, MOVING EVER WESTWARD.

ONE DAY THEY SEE THE BLEACHING RIBS OF A WRECKED SHIP WHICH THEY RECOGNIZE AS THAGNAR'S.

AND AMID THE WRECKAGE FIND BOLD THAGNAR'S HORNED HELMET.

82 9-4-38

FURTHER DIGGING REVEALS THAT WHICH THEY FEARED MOST TO FIND, A JEWELED CLASP,—ILENE'S!

TWO DESPERATELY UNHAPPY LADS FACE A WORL[D] NO LONGER MADE GAY BY THE BRIGHT HAIR AND LAUGHING EYES OF THE MAID THEY HA[VE] LOVED. *NEXT WEEK—HOMEWARD*

SYNOPSIS
ILENE OF THE HONEY-COLORED HAIR HAD GONE AND WITH HER ALL THE JOY AND HAPPINESS HER TWO PRINCELY LOVERS HAD KNOWN. THEY HAD FACED DEATH AND DANGER WITH A LAUGH, HARDSHIP WITH A SHRUG, BUT THE ENDING OF ALL THEIR DREAMS LEAVES THEM HEART-BROKEN AND BEWILDERED IN A LONELY WORLD

ON A LEDGE ABOVE THE WRECKED SHIP THEY BUILD A CAIRN TO THE MEMORY OF THE FAIR ILENE.

SILENTLY THEY TURN WESTWARD TO SEEK SOME WAY OF CROSSING THE ROUGH SEA THAT SEPARATES THEM FROM ENGLAND.

ONE STORMY DAY A WIDE RIVER-MOUTH BARS THEIR WAY

WHILE GATHERING DRIFTWOOD FOR A RAFT VAL SUDDENLY SHOUTS, "LOOK, A GREAT SHIP IS BEING DRIVEN TO DESTRUCTION BY THE WAVES."

»BUILD A SIGNAL FIRE TO ATTRACT THEIR ATTENTION, ARN, WHILE I SWIM ACROSS TO THE OTHER POINT.«

THE MARINERS SEE THEIR SIGNAL AND THE TWO BOYS GUIDE THE PITCHING VESSEL TO THE SAFETY OF THE RIVER-MOUTH.

"LOOK, ARN, KNIGHTS OF THE ROUND TABLE, SIR KAY, PERCIVAL, NEGARTH, TRISTRAM AND VRIENS. WE ARE SAVED !"

· NEXT WEEK ·
HOMEWARD BOUND

83 9-11-38

83

SYNOPSIS: THEIR QUEST FOR ILENE ENDS IN TRAGEDY AND THE TWO YOUNG PRINCES TURN UNHAPPILY HOMEWARD. BY GOOD FORTUNE THEY ARE ABLE TO GUIDE A STORM-TOSSED SHIP TO A SAFE HARBOR AND FIND FRIENDS FROM HOME ON BOARD.

THE GREAT SHIP COMES ROCKING IN FROM THE SEA AND DROPS ANCHOR.

A BOAT IS SENT ASHORE TO FETCH THE RESCUERS ABOARD

AND A WHOLEHEARTED WELCOME IS GIVEN THE TWO HAGGARD WANDERERS.

THE ONCE GAY AND WITTY VAL TELLS OF THEIR FRANTIC QUEST, ITS PITIFUL END AND THE WEARY RETURN.

"THE GLAD TIDINGS WE BRING MAY EASE YOUR SORROW," SAYS KINDLY SIR ECTOR, "FOR KING ARTHUR HAS DRIVEN THE ANGLES TO THE COAST AND MADE ENGLAND SAFE AGAIN."

"AND WE GO TO FETCH THE NOBLE SIR LAUNCELOT OUT OF BRITTANY TO ATTEND THE GREATEST TOURNAMENT IN HISTORY IN CELEBRATION OF THE VICTORY."

WHEN THE STORM ABATES THE GAY COMPANY SAILS UP THE COAST OF GAUL AND BRITTANY.

AND ENTERS THE HARBOR BENEATH THE FROWNING CASTLE OF KING BORS AND HIS SON, SIR LAUNCELOT.

84 9-18-38

BUT VAL AND ARN HAVE NO HEART FOR THE GAIETY WITHIN THE CASTLE THAT NIGHT.

NEXT WEEK — LAUNCELOT'S COUNSEL

SYNOPSIS: TOGETHER PRINCE ARN AND VAL HAVE SEARCHED WILD NORTHERN SEAS AND HOSTILE COASTS FOR NEWS OF ILENE, ONLY TO LEARN IN THE END THAT THEIR BELOVED HAS PERISHED IN A STORM. IN THE QUIET GARDENS SIR LAUNCELOT FINDS THE TWO DESPERATELY UNHAPPY LADS.

"DO NOT GRIEVE FOR ILENE — FATE HAS SPARED HER MUCH UNHAPPINESS."

"HAD SHE BEEN FOUND YOU WERE PLEDGED TO FIGHT TO THE DEATH FOR HER HAND; THE WINNER WOULD LIVE ON KNOWING HE HAD BOUGHT A BRIDE WITH HIS FRIEND'S LIFE, AND GENTLE ILENE WOULD BE THE WIFE OF A MURDERER, FOREVER BLAMING HERSELF FOR BEING THE CAUSE OF IT ALL."

"SIR LAUNCELOT IS RIGHT, ARN, AND OUR QUEST MIGHT HAVE ENDED EVEN MORE DISASTROUSLY."

AT DAWN THE STATELY WAR-SHIP LEAVES FOR ENGLAND AND THE GREAT TOURNAMENT.

SAILING UP THE SOLENT THEY LAND AND JOIN THE MARCH TO CAMELOT, A GAY LAUGHING TROOP.

"HERE I MUST LEAVE FOR MY FATHER'S KINGDOM AT ORD, BUT IN YOUR CARE I LEAVE THE CHARMED SINGING SWORD TO BE USED IN GOOD KING ARTHUR'S CAUSE."

85 9-25-38

MANY KNIGHTS THRONG THE ROADS UNTIL A SPLENDID PROCESSION WITH BANNERS FLYING AND TRUMPETS SOUNDING, MOVES ON TO CAMELOT, CITY OF WONDER.

· NEXT WEEK — KING ARTHUR ·

SYNOPSIS: RETURNING FROM HIS ADVENTURES OVERSEAS VAL TRAVELS IN COMPANY WITH MANY KNIGHTS TO CAMELOT WHERE SPLENDID PREPARATIONS ARE GOING FORWARD FOR THE GREAT TOURNAMENT.

BOISTEROUSLY GAY SIR GAWAIN WELCOMES HIS WANDERING SQUIRE!

PRINCE VALIANT IS HONORED BY THE KING'S INTEREST AND HE TELLS ARTHUR AND GUINEVERE OF HIS TRAGIC QUEST.

"AND NOW, SIRE," IMPLORES VAL, "GRANT ME SOME GREAT QUEST WHOSE FULFILLMENT WILL MAKE ME WORTHY OF KNIGHTHOOD, FOR I CRAVE FELLOWSHIP OF THE ROUND TABLE ABOVE ALL ELSE."

"YOU ARE BUT A LAD YET, PRINCE VALIANT," SAYS KING ARTHUR, "WHEN YOU HAVE GROWN STRONG ENOUGH TO CONTEND ON EQUAL TERMS WITH MY VETERAN KNIGHTS,—PERHAPS."

"PERHAPS IF I SPILL SOME OF HIS BEST KNIGHTS AT THE TOURNAMENT THE KING WILL TAKE NOTICE."

MIDNIGHT IN THE DESERTED ARMORY AND VAL GATHERS AND REPAIRS BITS OF ABANDONED ARMOR.

AND PAINTS ALL WHITE HIS ASSEMBLED ARMS— SIGN OF AN UNTRIED KNIGHT.

Copr. 1938. King Features Syndicate, Inc. World rights reserved   86 10-2-38

WHEN THE SPLENDID CONCOURSE OF KNIGHTS, THEIR LADIES AND RETAINERS LEAVE FOR CAERLEON AND THE GREAT TOURNAMENT, THE SILENT WHITE KNIGHT RIDES WITH THEM IN SECOND-HAND ARMOR, ON A BORROWED CHARGER.

—NEXT WEEK— "CAERLEON"

HAL FOSTER

Prince Valiant

SYNOPSIS: KING ARTHUR HAS HINTED THAT VAL IS TOO YOUNG TO CONTEND WITH VETERAN KNIGHTS. BUT, WITH THE CONFIDENCE OF YOUTH, VAL IN A SECOND HAND SUIT OF ARMOR ENTERS THE GREAT TOURNAMENT TO TRY FOR HIS GOLDEN SPURS.

VAL WAITS ALONE AND UNATTENDED FOR HE DARE NOT TRUST HIS FELLOW SQUIRES OR MEN-AT-ARMS, WHO ARE ENVIOUS OF HIS PRINCELY BEARING AND POPULARITY WITH THE KNIGHTS OF THE ROUND TABLE.

TRUMPETS SOUND AND A MIGHTY SHOUT GOES UP AS TWO HUNDRED BRILLIANT KNIGHTS SWING INTO THEIR SADDLES.

THEY FACE EACH OTHER IN TWO LONG LINES— KING ARTHUR GIVES THE SIGNAL —

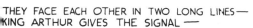

THE EARTH SHAKES WITH THE THUNDER OF HOOFS AND THE FIRST FLIGHT CRASHES TO VICTORY OR DEFEAT.

IT IS ROUGH AND DANGEROUS SPORT AND AT THE END OF THE FOURTH FLIGHT BUT TEN KNIGHTS ARE LEFT FOR THE CHALLENGE ROUND.

THESE TEN MAY CHALLENGE WHOM THEY PLEASE TO SINGLE COMBAT—TO THE ASTONISHMENT OF ALL THE WHITE KNIGHT TURNS TO THE PARK OF CHAMPIONS

AND STRIKES THE SHIELD OF TRISTRAM, GREATEST OF ALL WARRIORS SAVE ONLY LAUNCELOT, A CHALLENGE HAS BEEN GIVEN !

87 10-9-38

NEXT WEEK —
A LONG CHANCE

SYNOPSIS: IN SECOND-HAND ARMOR AND ON A BORROWED HORSE VAL ENTERS THE GREAT TOURNAMENT DETERMINED TO WIN HIS GOLDEN SPURS. FROM THE GRAND MELEE HE EMERGES ONE OF THE VICTORS — IMMEDIATELY HE CHALLENGES MIGHTY TRISTRAM TO SINGLE COMBAT.

THE NEXT FEW MINUTES WILL BRING VAL EITHER CRUSHING DEFEAT OR A CHANCE FOR KNIGHTHOOD.

"THIS UNKNOWN WHITE KNIGHT HAS MORE COURAGE THAN SENSE — FIND OUT WHO HE IS AND WHETHER HE WIN OR LOSE, BRING HIM HERE TO ME." SAYS THE KING.

THE TRICK OF THE SLANTING SHIELD DEFLECTS TRISTRAM'S LANCE AS HIS OWN IS SHATTERED BY THE IMPACT.

THERE IS AN EMBARRASSING PAUSE THEN A RIPPLE OF LAUGHTER FROM THE CROWD WHEN THEY REALIZE THE UNKNOWN KNIGHT OWNS BUT ONE LANCE. 88 10-16-38

BUT SIR GAWAIN HAS RIGHTLY GUESSED WHO THE WHITE KNIGHT REALLY IS — "HONOR ME BY USING MINE," HE SAYS, THEN WHISPERS, "YOU STOUT-HEARTED YOUNG IDIOT."

TRISTRAM IS NO LONGER SMILING. "BRING ME MY STOUTEST LANCE," HE ORDERS, "THIS NAMELESS UPSTART STRIKES LIKE A THUNDER-BOLT."

TRUMPETS SOUND AND AGAIN THE SIGNAL IS GIVEN!—
NEXT WEEK — LOUD LAUGHTER

Prince Valiant

IN THE DAYS OF KING ARTHUR
BY HAROLD R FOSTER

SYNOPSIS: TO WIN THE COVETED GOLDEN SPURS OF KNIGHTHOOD VAL ENTERS THE GREAT TOURNAMENT AND BATTLES HIS WAY TO THE CHALLENGE ROUND. HE STAKES ALL ON A SINGLE CHANCE AND SELECTS SIR TRISTRAM, ONE OF ENGLAND'S GREATEST KNIGHTS, FOR HIS FINAL OPPONENT. THE FIRST HEAD—LONG CHARGE ENDS IN A DRAW.

FOR THE SECOND TIME THE DARING YOUNG PRINCE AND THE MIGHTY KNIGHT GALLOP HEADLONG AT EACH OTHER.

TRISTRAM IS WELL—NIGH LIFTED FROM HIS SADDLE ERE VAL'S WEAPON SPLINTERS — HIS OWN STOUT LANCE HOLDS AND VAL AND HIS HORSE GO CRASHING TO DEFEAT.

THE SHOCK RIPS VAL'S HELMET FROM HIS HEAD AND DISCLOSES THE IDENTITY OF THE WHITE KNIGHT.

LOUD JEERS RING OUT FROM HIS FELLOW SQUIRES AS VAL IS RECOGNIZED, FOR THEY ARE ENVIOUS OF HIS POPULARITY WITH THE KNIGHTS.

89 10-23-38

DAZEDLY VAL WALKS FROM THE FIELD AMID A THUNDER OF APPLAUSE.

"MAY I NEVER HAVE TO MEET THAT YOUNG SPITFIRE AGAIN," SAYS TRISTRAM, "I ACHE ALL OVER FROM HIS BLOWS."

"WHY, IT WAS YOUNG PRINCE VALIANT WHO WELL—NIGH UNSEATED THE MIGHTY TRISTRAM," EXCLAIMS THE KING. "BRING HIM TO ME."

Copr. 1938, King Features Syndicate, Inc., World rights reserved.

BUT VAL' HEARD ONLY THE JEERS OF THE SQUIRES AND THINKS THE WHOLE ENSEMBLAGE IS LAUGHING AT HIS PRESUMPTION. QUIETLY HE LEAVES CAERLEON.
NEXT WEEK—HOME TO THE FENS

Prince Valiant
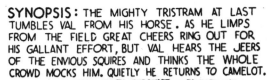
IN THE DAYS OF KING ARTHUR
BY HAROLD R FOSTER

SYNOPSIS: THE MIGHTY TRISTRAM AT LAST TUMBLES VAL FROM HIS HORSE. AS HE LIMPS FROM THE FIELD GREAT CHEERS RING OUT FOR HIS GALLANT EFFORT, BUT VAL HEARS THE JEERS OF THE ENVIOUS SQUIRES AND THINKS THE WHOLE CROWD MOCKS HIM. QUIETLY HE RETURNS TO CAMELOT.

THE YOUNG PRINCE IS DEEPLY HURT BY THE FANCIED MOCKERY.

AS FIRST HE CAME TO CAMELOT SO NOW DOES HE LEAVE, RICHER ONLY BY HIS POSSESSION OF THE SINGING SWORD,

AND TURNS HIS STEPS TOWARD THE PEACE AND QUIET OF HIS OLD HOME IN THE MYSTERIOUS FENS.

BY THE EDGE OF THE GREAT MARSH HE MEETS AGAIN HIS BOYHOOD FRIEND.

THE YOUNG SHEPHERD AGREES TO TAKE CARE OF VAL'S MOUNTS.

TO HIS GREAT JOY VAL FINDS HIS OLD DUGOUT STILL IN ITS HIDING-PLACE.

WITH MELTED RESIN AND CHARCOAL HE REPAIRS THE CRACKS.

ONCE AGAIN HE DRIVES HIS SLENDER CANOE SWIFTLY THROUGH THE MAZE OF CHANNELS,—HIS SPIRITS RISING IN THE FREEDOM OF THE FAMILIAR SWAMPS.

HAL FOSTER

AFTER TWO YEARS OF WANDERING VAL ONCE MORE APPROACHES THE ISLAND WHERE HIS KINGLY FATHER LIVES IN EXILE.

90 10-30-38

WHILE AT COURT THE KING COMMANDS—"BRING ME PRINCE VALIANT THAT HE MAY BE KNIGHTED STRONGER WARRIORS THERE MAY BE, BUT NONE MORE BRAVE OR SKILLFUL!" NEXT WEEK: FUTURE PLANS

SYNOPSIS: AFTER NEARLY TWO YEARS OF ADVENTUROUS WANDERINGS PRINCE VAL RETURNS TO HIS HOME IN THE FENS, WHERE HIS FATHER, THE EXILED KING OF THULE, LIVES WITH A HANDFUL OF FAITHFUL WARRIORS.

AS HE SETS FOOT ON THE ISLAND VAL TAKES A DEEP BREATH AND SHOUTS FOR JOY.

FROM THE GATEWAY COMES AN ANSWERING SHOUT— "PRINCE VALIANT HAS RETURNED TO US! WELCOME, VAL."

AND THE AGING VETERANS CROWD AROUND THE STALWART YOUNG WARRIOR WHO HAD LEFT THEM AS A BOY.

SHOUTING LUSTILY THEY HURRY TO THE LOW RAFTERED HALL WHERE THE KING, HIS FACE BEAMING WITH PLEASURE, RISES TO WELCOME HIS DARING SON.

BEFORE THE GREAT FIREPLACE VAL RECOUNTS HIS STORY TO THE KING.

ONCE MORE THE HUNTER, VAL ROAMS FAR AND FREE ACROSS HIS BELOVED FENS.

THE OLD FASCINATION OF THE GREAT WASTE COMES BACK AND HOLDS HIM — FOR A WHILE HE IS CONTENT.

91 11-6-38

BUT, AFTER THE CLASH OF BATTLES AND THE HIGH ADVENTURINGS OF KING ARTHUR'S COURT THIS IS BUT CHILD'S PLAY. WHILE WINTER WINDS HOWL MOURNFULLY AROUND THE HOUSE VAL LAYS GREAT PLANS FOR THE FUTURE.

·NEXT WEEK·
AGAIN THE WITCH!

SYNOPSIS: WHEN HE TOLD HIS FATHER THE STORY OF HIS ADVENTURES VAL DID NOT TELL THE EXILED KING OF HIS MEETING WITH SLIGON; THE TYRANT WHO HAD USURPED THE THRONE OF THULE — NOW HE PLANS TO REGAIN THE LOST KINGDOM AND FREE THE PEOPLE FROM OPPRESSION. WITH THIRTY AGING WARRIORS HE WOULD CONQUER AN ARMY!

FAR OFF IN THE HEART OF THE FENS LIVES HORRIT, THE WITCH WHO HAD PROPHESIED ALL TOO TRULY THE TRAGEDIES OF VAL'S LIFE. TO HER VAL WOULD GO AGAIN FOR COUNSEL.

WHEN BITTER JANUARY WINDS HOLD TIGHT THE GREAT SWAMP IN AN ICY GRIP VAL SPEEDS ON HIS MISSION.

FANTASTIC NORTHERN LIGHTS DANCE WEIRDLY ACROSS THE STILL NIGHT AS HE REACHES THE BLEAK HOVEL.

HORRIT AND HER HIDEOUS SON SCREAM IN TERROR AT VAL'S UNEXPECTED INTRUSION.

"I BRING FOOD AND A WARM CLOAK AS GIFTS, NOW TELL ME WHAT A MAN MAY ACCOMPLISH WITH THE SINGING SWORD?"

"HIDE THAT ACCURSED BLADE FROM MY SIGHT," WAILS THE WITCH, "THAT IS THE CHARMED SWORD, FLAMBERGE, MADE BY THE SAME MAGE WHO FORGED KING ARTHUR'S EXCALIBUR!"

"NO KEENER BLADE WAS EVER WROUGHT AND TO ITS OWNER WILL COME HARD VICTORY, IF HE FIGHT. WITH A PURE HEART AND IN A GOOD CAUSE. BUT WOE TO HIM WHO USES IT FOR EVIL GAIN! GET RID OF IT, PRETTY BOY, FOR IT IS A TERRIBLE MASTER!" THEN SHE PROPHESIES WHAT MAY NOT BE TOLD HERE, BUT VAL IS WHITE AND TREMBLING WHEN —

92 11-13-38

HAL FOSTER

HE EMERGES INTO THE THIN, COLD DAWN AND FLEES HOMEWARD, SHIVERING WITH DREAD —
NEXT WEEK — THIN ICE